MW00805864

# Provence

## Portraits of France©

**Photos** Vincent Formica
**Text** David Fréchet
**Translation** Susan Pickford

**Origination and editorial direction** Bertrand Dalin

Warmest thanks to the following, without whose precious and much appreciated help this book would not have been possible: Liliane Counord, René Bruni, Michel Del Burgo, Jean-André Charial, M. and Mme. Denis Ceccon, Muriel Botella, and Sylvie Sesenta —not forgetting Joachim and Virginie at La Bouteillerie.

*Front cover - The beautiful colours of the village of Roussillon glow red in the evening sun against the stunning backdrop of Mont Ventoux.*

*Preceding double spread - The astonishing sight of rows of lavender stretching to the horizon, hugging the curves of the hill like a striped purple dress.*

# Contents



*Preceding page - It is clear why Provence has always inspired artists. Every bend in the road reveals a picturesque tableau.*

*An almond tree floating like a cloud of whipped cream on the intense purple of a lavender field—a typical Provençal scene that is a treat for the nose as well as the eyes.*

# Editorial

Provence is a land of water: washed by the waters of the Mediterranean and by the majestic Rhône, while the marshy salt flats of the Camargue stretch to the west. It is a land of air: the mistral that drives men mad, sucks the moisture from the bone-dry plains, and flirts with the flowered skirts of the belles Provençales.

It is a land of earth: arid and stony on the Crau plateau, lush brown in the Comtat plain, in all shades of orange, tan, and saffron in the ochre mines of Roussillon, or on the slopes of Mont Ventoux.

It is a land of fire: the warmth of the sun that pours over the landscape until it glows like honey, devastating orange flames that make the tinder-dry pines explode like fireworks.

These four elements are the keys to the treasures that Provence offers so bountifully.

Explore the magic of Provence!

*Preceding page - A magnificent sunset over Mont Ventoux, the "giant of Provence".*

*The village of Saignon, in the Lubéron, caressed by the warmth of the morning sun.*

# History

In administrative terms, Provence is defined as the six départements of Alpes-de-Haute-Provence, Hautes-Alpes, Alpes-Maritimes, Bouches-du-Rhône, Var, and Vaucluse. Yet the region is so alive with history that it is a shame to see it purely in terms of political geography. The Provençal lifestyle reaches as far as the Drôme and the Gard. To ignore these areas would be to leave out part of the soul of Provence.

This book covers the Provence described by the nineteenth-century poet Frédéric Mistral as "between sea, Rhône and Durance", from Montélimar in the north to Marseilles and the Riviera, from the Rhône valley to the foothills of the Alps, from the high plateaux of the Var to the Verdon gorges. The region has many tales to tell about its rich history: the first human settlement here dates back some seven hundred thousand years.

*Preceding page - The Arles arena by moonlight: a reminder that Provence was once part of the Roman Empire.*

*Good King René ruled over Provence from 1434 to 1480. This statue on the cours Mirabeau in Aix-en-Provence, King René's capital, was sculpted by David d'Angers.*

Provence is one of the cradles of humanity. Palaeontologists have found traces of pre-Neanderthal activity in the Vaucluse from the lower Palaeolithic to the Tertiary period.

Our pre-human ancestors lived in caves near Bédoin and Mormoiron or among the boulders scattered on the flanks of Mont Ventoux, where fossil dinosaur eggs have also recently been discovered. The long tale of human evolution is illustrated in the region by unimaginably ancient paintings of animals on the walls of a cave in Cosquer, between Marseilles and Cassis.

*The gorges carved in the living rock over millennia by the river Verdon are a grandiose site.*

*Following page - Bories in a field of lavender. These dry-stone huts are a relic of the earliest human settlements in Provence.*

Gradually, over thousands upon thousands of years, men began to build permanent settlements in the region, consisting of groups of rudimentary huts. They learnt how to farm plants and herd animals. The Ligurians were the dominant tribe until, in the fifth century B.C., the Greeks arrived, founding Massilia (now Marseilles) and colonising the coastline from Agde to Monaco.

In the fourth century B.C., Celtic peoples from central Europe migrated to the region and intermarried with local tribes, forming powerful clans: the Tricastins round Saint-Paul-Trois-Châteaux, the Voconces from les Baronnies to Sisteron, the Albii round Sault and the Lubéron, the Cavares in the rest of the Vaucluse, and the Salyens between the Lubéron and the Mediterranean and from the Rhône to the Var.

*Preceding page - The triumphal arch in Orange is a reminder of the days when Provence was a prosperous Roman colony.*

*The Roman theatre in Arles is rich in history, and still plays an important role in the life of the town today.*

The period of Roman colonisation brought great wealth to the region. The Romans founded Aquae Sextiae (now Aix-en-Provence) as the capital of this outpost of the great empire, which they called Provincia Romana—hence the name Provence.

Under the Emperor Augustus, the Romans extended their domination in the region as far as Arles, Vaison-la-Romaine, Orange, Cavaillon, and Saint-Rémy-de-Provence. All of these towns have a rich heritage of Roman ruins dating from the first and second centuries A.D. This prosperous period lasted until the third century A.D., when the region was overrun by hordes of invading Germanic barbarians. The Emperor Constantine withdrew to Arles, which was one of the jewels of the Roman Empire before becoming the capital of the Gauls. From the third century A.D., Christianity increasingly gained ground in Provence. Bishoprics and monasteries were founded throughout the region.

*The mausoleum of the Julius family, related to Caesar, and the triumphal arch in Saint-Rémy-de-Provence.*

*The Roman bridge in Vaison-la-Romaine.*

*Following page - A cryptoporticus, or enclosed gallery, dating from the first century B.C., found beneath the Jesuit chapel in Arles.*

After the fall of the Roman Empire in 476 A.D., Provence once again fell prey to barbarian hordes of Visigoths, Ostrogoths and Burgundians, until the Ostrogoth King Vitiges ceded his territory to Clovis, King of the Franks, in 536.

Under Carolingian rule, Provence was just a small part of the immense empire that Charlemagne left to his heirs, Lothar and Charles the Bald. When Charles the Bald died in 879, his brother-in-law Boson had himself declared king of Provence by the local lords and bishops. He thereby founded an independent local dynasty that reigned until the late fifteenth century. In fact, southern Provence was governed by three successive dynasties: the Bosonides (879-1112), the Catalans (1112-1246), and the Angevins (1246-1481).

*The portal of the church of Saint-Trophime in Arles, a masterpiece of Romanesque architecture.*

*Following page - The oldest parts of the Château d'Ansouis in the Lubéron date back to the tenth century. It has been in the Sabran family since 961. The descendants of this old Provençal dynasty still live here.*

Under the Bosonides, Provence was part of the kingdom of Arles, before being ceded to Rodolphe II of Burgundy. On the death of Rodolphe III, Provence and Burgundy both became part of the Holy Roman Empire, although the counts of Provence still held the reins of power.

Part of Provence was at this time occupied by the Saracens. The land they held was liberated in 972 by Guillaume I, Count of Arles, known as the Liberator.

In 1112, Douce, the last of the Boson dynasty, married Raimond Bérenger I, Count of Barcelona, bringing Provence as her dowry. This led to hostilities between the counts of Barcelona and the counts of Toulouse, and it soon became clear that part of Provence would have to be relinquished to settle the dispute. On September 15th, 1125, a treaty was signed, dividing Provence between the two powers. The Count of Barcelona held on to lower Provence, from south of the river Durance to the Mediterranean, while the Count of Toulouse gained territories north of the Durance (including what is now the Comtat Venaissin) and the right bank of the Rhône round Argence and Beaucaire. A third county was formed at Forcalquier, and Avignon remained undivided.

*Preceding page - The broken bridge in Avignon, known to children everywhere from the song "Sur le pont d'Avignon".*

*The Palais des Papes in Avignon is the largest Gothic building in all Europe.*

The twelfth century was the golden age of Provençal Romanesque architecture. Countless small churches were built in towns and villages throughout the region, along with grander cathedrals and abbeys such as the Benedictine abbey of Montmajour and the Cistercian abbeys in Sénanque and Silvacane.

Relations between the counts of Barcelona and Toulouse remained stormy until the mid-thirteenth century, when in 1246, Charles I, Count of Anjou, the future King of Naples and brother of Saint Louis, King of France, married Béatrix, daughter of Raimond Bérenger V, Count of Barcelona. Like Douce before her, she too brought her new husband Provence as her dowry. The region remained part of the first House of Anjou until 1380, when Charles I's heir, Queen Jeanne, having no children of her own, adopted Louis I, Duke of Anjou. Provence remained in the possession of this second House of Anjou for another century.

*The village of Bédoin, at the foot of Mont Ventoux, has a most impressive church in the Jesuit style.*

The fourteenth century was a period of schism in the Catholic church. From 1309 to 1403, the papacy was based in Avignon. The seven popes and two antipopes who ruled Christendom from the Palais des Papes made Avignon the commercial and artistic heart of Europe, bringing wealth to the region by building residences for the popes and cardinals in Villneuve-lès-Avignon, Malaucène, Barbentane, and Châteauneuf-du-Pape.

The history of the fifteenth century is dominated by the towering figure of Good King René, whose long reign (1434-1480) marked a golden age for Provence, bringing prosperity and peace, especially for his new capital, Aix-en-Provence.

On King René's death in 1480, the county of Provence passed to his nephew Charles of Maine. The new king died just a year later, and in his will, dated December 10th, 1481, he bequeathed the county to King Louis XI. All Provence thus became part of France, excepting the principality of Orange which became French in 1731, and the Comtat Venaissin and Avignon which retained independence until 1791.

*The Cistercian abbey in Sénanque is a fine example of the Romanesque style, typical of Provençal architecture from the twelfth century onwards.*

From the late fifteenth to the late eighteenth century, the region was ruled as the absolutist States of Provence. It was a period of unprecedented prosperity, both in the urban centres and in rural areas. The traditional Provençal style of architecture, for example, developed as a result of the construction of large bastides, or country residences, where the local aristocracy would spend the summer on their farmlands.

Although the region was torn by religious strife and regular epidemics, such as a major outbreak of plague in 1720, the towns of Provence grew rapidly in size. The rapid population growth was accompanied by an equally spectacular economic boom, which played an important role in the development of the towns. The cours Mirabeau in Aix-en-Provence and the cours Belsunce in Marseilles, for example, were planned broad enough for the coaches of the wealthy aristocrats who built so many fine private residences there.

*Preceding page - The quiet charm of a little Romanesque chapel set in a field of wild flowers.*

*A superb carved wooden door belonging to one of the numerous sumptuous town residences built for the local aristocracy in Aix in the seventeenth and eighteenth centuries.*

The impact of the 1789 revolution was felt as strongly here as everywhere else in France. There were peasant uprisings in the countryside and riots in Aix, Arles, and Avignon. In 1791, the revolutionaries in Avignon formed the "Vaucluse army" (even before the Vaucluse officially existed) and attacked the Comtat Venaissin, which had remained faithful to the papacy.

In September that same year, the revolutionary Constitutive Assembly declared Avignon and the Comtat to be "an integral part of the French Empire", and the département of the Vaucluse was formed in 1793. However, the pope only formally agreed to abandon his claim to these territories in 1797.

*The village of Châteauneauf-du-Pape and its vineyards are a byword for great wine all over the world.*

The nineteenth century saw profound upheavals in the traditional Provençal way of life, thanks to the improvement of transport and communication links with the birth of the industrial era, and in particular the introduction of two new sources of wealth: olive trees and vines. An efficient system of irrigation was installed on the Comtat plain, which, together with the fertile land along both banks of the river Durance, began to supply fruit and vegetables to the whole region. Modern industries developed all the way along the Rhône valley to Marseilles, which specialised in industries relying on imported raw materials.

The Second Empire (1852-1870) witnessed the birth of a flourishing literary movement which played a major role in awakening interest in the history of Provence. The Félibrige movement was founded in the village of Châteauneuf-de-Gadagne, near Avignon, in 1854, by seven poets and writers, all natives of Provence. The most famous of these founding members was Frédéric Mistral, whose poetic oeuvre is a hymn to the beauties of his homeland.

*Frédéric Mistral was a Provençal poet and founding member of the Félibrige movement. He was born in Maillane in 1830. This statue is in the place du Forum in Arles.*

Agriculture has remained an important sector of the Provençal economy throughout the twentieth century and into the twenty-first. Wine production has been of particular importance, and in the last few decades côtes-du-rhône wines have made enormous strides in terms of quality and reputation.

Tourism has also been an important source of revenue. The authorities have made great efforts to develop the region's reputation as a cultural centre and keep the local festivals alive. Tourism and culture are now the biggest source of jobs, and Provence's position as a tourist destination is solidly established.

Now, at the beginning of the twenty-first century, a new high-speed train line has brought Marseilles and Avignon within three hours of Paris.

Provence has everything to offer visitors: the Mediterranean on their doorstep, a delightful climate, varied and bountiful landscapes, picturesque villages, and areas of outstanding natural beauty. Small wonder that Provence now has the fastest growing population of any region in Europe.

*Preceding page - The windmill in Fontvieille was immortalised by Alphonse Daudet in his book Letters from my Windmill.*

*The superb curves of Avignon's brand new train station, designed by the architects Jean-François Blassel and Jean-Marie Duthilleul. The building was inaugurated in 2001.*

Coutellerie

# Towns and villages

A shady town square lined with plane trees, a stone fountain, a chapel with a tall bell tower, a courtyard with a beaten earth track where a game of petanque is being hotly disputed by a group of elderly men. The metallic click of the bowls echoes the rhythmical sawing of the cicadas.

This is what tourists imagine to be the essence of a typical Provençal village. While it sounds like a cliché, it is a scene that is to be found time and time again in villages throughout this delightful region, from the south of the Drôme to the thyme-scented countryside of the upper Var.

*Preceding page - The village of Aups in the uplands of the Var. A typical Provençal scene: a square with shady café terraces and a fountain in the centre.*

*The bell tower in Aups, glimpsed through a stone archway.*

Let's begin, as so many visitors do, by arriving from the north. Provence begins in the Drôme, where the rolling green fields of the Dauphiné give way to more typically southern vegetation. Once past Montélimar and the Donzère canyon, the difference becomes striking: on the long drive down from Paris, it is a favourite game to look out for the first olive tree, the first cypress, holm oak, and evergreen kermes oak, the first house with ochre-washed walls and a curved tiled roof.

Soon we are in the Tricastin region, with its stone-walled villages: Le Garde-Adhémar perched on a rocky outcrop, Saint-Restitut peeking out from a pine plantation, Suze-la-Rousse overshadowed by its powerful feudal château, and, of course, Grignan, dear to the heart of the Comtesse de Sévigné, who wrote countless letters to her beloved daughter who owned a superb Renaissance château there.

*Montbrun-les-Bains is counted among the loveliest villages in France.*

*Aurel is an isolated rural community in the Vaucluse near the town of Sault.*

*Following page - The village of Reilhanette in the south of the Baronnies.*

Here, straddling the Drôme and the Vaucluse uplands, we are well and truly in Provence. We could make a short detour to visit a curious relic of French history—the Enclave des Papes, a small part of the Vaucluse that is now an enclave in the Drôme. It gets its name—and peculiar status—from the fact that it was once a papal possession when the papacy was in Avignon. It is home to four villages: Valréas, Visan, Grillon, and Richerenches, celebrated for its truffle market and its historical links with the Knights Templar.

Further east, we are back in the Drôme, crossing le Nyonsais and les Baronnies. The town of Nyons has a beautiful historic centre and a square, the Place aux Herbes, which has retained its medieval atmosphere. It is also famed for its microclimate, perfect for growing olives. This is the furthest north olives will mature.

*Preceding page - A view of Monieux, near Sault, by night.*

*The village of Brantes, in the Vaucluse, on the north side of Mont Ventoux, where the Pre-Alps begin.*

The landscape of les Baronnies is more rugged. The rolling hills stretch into the distance and eventually grow into the Alps. The villages nestled on the hillsides and in the valleys have charmingly evocative names: Mérindol-les-Oliviers, Mirabel-aux-Baronnies, La Roche-sous-le-Buis, and the regional capital, Buis-les-Baronnies, which has a magnificent old market place edged with fifteenth-century arcades. It also hosts an annual Lime Tree Fair held in July beneath the plane trees that line the banks of the river Ouvèze.

To the east, close to where the Drôme finishes and Haute-Provence begins, the villages cling to rockier slopes between the north face of Mont Ventoux and the Montagne de Lure: Séderon, Monbrun-les-Bains (so called because people once came to take the sulphurous waters of the local cold springs), Reilhanette—a delightfully musical name—and further towards Vaucluse, the villages of Aurel, Brantes, and Monieux. Let's continue our route through the uplands of Vaucluse, scattered with tiny villages, each more charming than the one before: Entrechaux, Mormoiron, Bédoin, Flassan. Each is a picturesque little gem.

Let's pause for a while in le Barroux, to the west of Mont Ventoux. The village stands under the shadow of a Renaissance fortress. The terrace offers a fabulous panoramic view as far as the Dentelles de Montmirail hills, the Comtat plain, and the Alpilles mountains.

*Le Barroux stands in the shadow of a magnificent Renaissance fortress.*

*Following page - Flassan is a picturesque village. The ochre-washed houses are typical of Provence.*

We could also halt near Vaison-la-Romaine, where the villages of Sablet and Séguret, on facing hills, seem to be no more than reflections of each other. These medieval villages, with their old stone houses and historic buildings dating from the twelfth to fifteenth centuries, are well worth visiting.

There can be nothing more charming than whiling away an hour or two on a sunny afternoon exploring their narrow streets, some of which are covered over by soustets, or traditional vaulted passageways.

*Preceding page and above - Sablet and Séguret, twin villages perched on facing hillsides near Vaison-la-Romaine.*

Vaison-la-Romaine itself is a pretty town where past and present meet in the bustling streets, in the Roman theatre and the numerous other ruins worthy of Pompeii in the Villasse and Puymin districts, in the upper part of town with its paved streets and treasures of medieval architecture, in the fifteenth-century cathedral, and in the ruins of the twelfth-century fortress built by the Counts of Toulouse on the summit of the rock that stands proudly over the town.

Among the numerous smaller towns that are scattered through Provence like polka dots on a skirt, one of the most delightful is surely L'Isle-sur-la-Sorgue, known locally as the Venice of the Comtat. The poet René Char was born here. The various branches of the river Sorgue encircle and pass through the heart of the town, powering enormous paddle wheels that are a reminder of the times when the town depended for its survival on its sixty or so paper and spinning mills. The names of certain streets—rue de l'Anguille (Eel street), rue de l'Ecrevisse (Crayfish street), rue de la Truite (Trout street)—are a reminder that this was once also a fishing village. It has become a paradise for bargain hunters, thanks to its numerous antiques dealers and its flea market.

*Preceding page - Vaison-la-Romaine has a lovely old medieval quarter dominated by the ruins of a twelfth-century fortress.*

*Watching the world go by from a riverside café terrace in L'Isle-sur-la-Sorgue.*

If we take the Route Nationale 100 out of L'Isle-sur-la-Sorgue heading east, we come to Apt. On the north side of the road are the mountains of Vaucluse, and to the south lies the Lubéron. On either side of the road are the prettiest of villages.

One of the best known is Gordes, officially classified one of the loveliest villages in France. It is a great favourite with tourists, among whom have been some celebrities. François Mitterrand, the former French president, the artists Chagall and Vasarely, and the photographer Willy Ronis all had homes there.

*Murs, to the north of Gordes, has a fine château dating from the fifteenth and sixteenth centuries. Brave Crillon, King Henri IV's comrade-in-arms, was born here.*

*Following page - Gordes is perched high on a hilltop, facing the Lubéron.*

The houses descend gracefully down the hill in terraced rows. On the summit stands a Renaissance-style château, which in parts betrays its medieval roots. South of Gordes is a curious little hamlet consisting of twenty or so bories, traditional round or conical dry-stone dwellings.

*Preceding page - A rare view of Gordes by night, with a light powdering of snow.*

*A dry-stone mazet set in a lonely field in the Vaucluse.*

Among the other villages honoured by inclusion in the list of the loveliest villages in France, several are in the Vaucluse: Venasque, Ménerbes, Roussillon, and further south, in the pays d'Aigues region, Lourmarin and Ansouis. Each of these villages is a superb showcase of traditional Provençal architecture and douceur de vivre.

Ménerbes was a stronghold for Calvinists during the wars of religion that tore southern France apart in the sixteenth century. The church offers a splendid view over the Lubéron and the Vaucluse mountains. The quality of the light and the tranquillity of the atmosphere have inspired a number of artists, including Nicolas de Staël who purchased the Castellet fortress, and Picasso, who came to stay with his muse Dora Maar in 1946.

*Preceding page - Roussillon is often called the most beautiful village in France.*

*Ansouis, between the Lubéron and the pays d'Aigues, has one of the finest châteaux in all Provence, home to the Sabran family since the twelfth century.*

*Since the 1920s, the Château de Lourmarin has been a foundation for artists, like the Villa Médicis in Rome.*

*Following page - The village of Lourmarin was home to the authors Henri Bosco and Albert Camus.*

The theatre director Jean Vilar called the village of Roussillon "Red Delphi". It is indeed a magical sight. The house façades are all in different shades of ochre, from honey tones to caramel browns to the red of a blood orange. The ochre is mined in quarries just outside the village. Samuel Beckett was among those to be seduced by Roussillon's stunning setting. He stayed here while writing his masterpiece Waiting for Godot, and it is said he helped with the grape harvest for the local côtes-du-lubéron vintage.

Many other artists and writers have succumbed to the charms of Provence, seeking calm and inspiration in one of the local villages. Henri Bosco and Albert Camus both chose to live in Lourmarin; both now repose in the cemetery there. Lourmarin is also well known for its majestic Renaissance château, which was acquired in the 1920s by an artistic foundation. It is now known familiarly as the Provençal Villa Médicis, in reference to the villa in Rome which regularly invites internationally renowned artists for study visits.

Many of the less well known villages in Lubéron are also worth a visit, and are likely to be less crowded by hordes of tourists. Lacoste stands in the shadow of the ruins of the Marquis de Sade's castle, now the property of the fashion designer Pierre Cardin.

Bonnieux has a lovely medieval church and unusual spiral ramparts. Saignon is perched perilously on a hillside. Visitors can inspect the ruins of no fewer than three thirteenth-century castles there. Its Romanesque church, clock tower, and the pretty place de la Fontaine make it one of the most enchanting villages in all Provence—among some very stiff competition.

*Preceding page - The houses of Bonnieux, in the heart of the Lubéron, seem to cascade higgledy-piggledy down the hillside. A medieval church stands guard over the village.*

*This old cart has found a new lease of life as the decorative centrepiece of a village square.*

Before we leave Vaucluse, we should pay a visit to the regional capital. Avignon, with its Italianate architecture, was truly worthy to be the seat of the popes when religious schisms drove them out of the Vatican in the fourteenth century. The Palais des Papes is the largest Gothic building in Europe. And of course, generations of children have sung the song "Sur le pont d'Avignon".

Just down the road is the town of Orange, founded by the Romans, who built what today is the best preserved Roman theatre anywhere in the world. Orange also boasts a triumphal arch, also miraculously intact, built in the early years of the 1st century A.D. to the glory of Julius Caesar.

Carpentras and Cavaillon are also interesting to visit, with their centuries-old reputation as the market gardens of Provence, supplying fruit and vegetables to the whole region. They also have a rich Jewish heritage. Carpentras has the oldest synagogue in France, dating from the fifteenth century, while Cavaillon has an eighteenth-century synagogue and a small museum devoted to local Jewish history.

*Preceding page - Above Apt, the tiny village of Saignon seems to cling to the bare rock face.*

*An old hand-painted advertisement on a house front in Carpentras.*

Past Cavaillon and beyond the river Durance, the part of Provence that stretches all the way to the Mediterranean is just as rich in picturesque villages and historic towns. Saint-Rémy and Les Baux-de-Provence, in the heart of the secretive, majestic Alpilles, are two fine examples. Saint-Rémy dates from the fourth century B.C., as attested by the Roman ruins of Glanum, once a thriving, bustling town, that share the same site.

Les Baux-de-Provence was founded in the eleventh century A.D., back in the days when the lords of Baux were among the most powerful feudal aristocrats in the south of France. On a promontory overlooking the village stand the ruins of their château. It offers a superb panoramic view over the town of Arles and the imposing abbey of Montmajour, the Crau plain, and the Camargue.

*Poppies are scattered like rubies in almost every field in Provence.*

*Following page: Les Baux-de-Provence is in a breath-taking natural site, high in the Alpilles.*

MORT À L'EMPIRE

Time has also woven a rich and varied tapestry in the town of Arles, whose streets are full of historic monuments and curiosities. The Roman Empire left behind an arena and theatre in what became the capital of the Gauls after the fall of the Roman Empire. There is also a superb Romanesque heritage in the shape of the portal and cloister of the church of Saint-Trophime, the most famous in all Provence.

The early days of Christianity are represented by the Alyscamps, considered by many one of the finest examples of an early necropolis, dating from the third to the seventh century. Fast forward to the nineteenth century, when the poor, tormented Vincent Van Gogh lived here between 1888 and 1890. He painted over three hundred masterpieces here, including L'Arlésienne, Le Pont de l'Anglois (The Anglois Bridge), Les Alyscamps, Le Café de Nuit (Night Café), and the famous Maison Jaune (Yellow House) where he lived.

*Preceding page: The Roman heart of Arles stretches along the banks of the Rhône.*

*A street corner in Arles, unchanged from the days when Vincent Van Gogh lived and painted here.*

Aix-en-Provence was home to another painter of genius. Paul Cézanne was born there in 1839 and studied law there before leaving for Paris and glory. He often returned home, never tiring of painting the Mont Sainte-Victoire. His studio was left untouched when he died in 1906, and is now a small museum.

Aix-en-Provence has a royal history, as it was capital of Provence in the days of good King René. The city centre has a rich heritage of historic buildings. Most of the centre has been closed off to vehicles, and there is no better way to discover the city than a stroll along the cours Mirabeau.

Just along the coast is Marseilles, the second largest city in France—and the oldest. From the old harbour and the Canebière, an avenue stretching through the heart of the city to the Panier district, from the district of Belle-de-Mai to the church of Notre-Dame-de-la-Garde, there are a thousand things to see and do. A boat trip round the calanques is also warmly recommended.

*Preceding page - The cours Mirabeau in Aix-en-Provence and the monumental fountain.*

*Cassis, a stone's throw from Marseilles, has a charming small fishing port. At night, the quayside twinkles with hundreds of lights.*

Moving inland from Marseilles, we come to the thyme-scented hills of the Var and Haute-Provence. Our route takes us to Cotignac and Aups in the upper Var, between Brignoles and the gorges of the river Verdon. The villages here are the very soul of Provence.

Cotignac is in a most spectacular site, backing onto a cliff eighty metres high. The entrance to the village is delightful, and the square in the heart of the village, with the village hall, fountain, and church belfry, is just as charming. The church Saint-Pierre, dating from the thirteenth to the seventeenth centuries, is also worth a look. It has a fabulous altar by Pierre Puget, a son of Marseilles and one of the greatest French sculptors of the seventeenth century.

*A sculpted stone fountain in a square in Cotignac, in the upper Var.*

*Following page - Aiguines, on the shores of Lac de Sainte-Croix,between the Var and Alpes-de-Haute-Provence*

We now head off to the Lac de Sainte-Croix, on the border between the départements of the Var and Alpes-de-Haute-Provence. Perched above the lake at an altitude of 820 metres, Aiguines is the northernmost village in the Var. Surrounded by a forest of box trees, it was once famed for its wood turners. A fascinating museum in the village tells the story of this local industry. Aiguines also has a Renaissance château with varnished roof tiles, and a pretty little church which is typically Provençal in character.

On the far shore of the lake, the département of Alpes-de-Haute-Provence begins. Seen from afar at night, when all the windows are lit up, the village of Moustiers-Sainte-Marie, with its huddle of houses and its bell tower, looks just like a Christmas crib scene. It was here that the now famous traditional Provence earthenware pottery was first made in the late seventeenth century by the artist Pierre Clérissy. In the eighteenth century, the village was home to around fifty master potters.

*A charmingly old-fashioned ironmonger's shop in Cotignac.*

*Following page - Moustiers-Sainte-Marie by night, resembling a Christmas crib scene.*

To the west, the plateau of Valensole takes us back towards the Lubéron. We shall pause for a short while in Gréoux-les-Bains, a little spa town reputed for its sulphurous water which works wonders for rheumatic joints. The ruins of a château of the Knights Templar on the summit of an Iron Age fortified site stand guard over the valley, carved out over countless thousands of years by the river Verdon.

*Preceding page - Nestled at the foot of an impressive rock face, Moustiers-Sainte-Marie greets the new day.*

*A typical Provençal fountain in Gréoux-les-Bains, an enchanting little spa town high above the Verdon gorges.*

Manosque is a busy little town, with its lively, shady squares lined with cafés and shops round the central fountain, and its lovely old houses.

All that remains standing of the ramparts that once defended the town from attack are two fortified gateways. Seen from the air, the line of the former ramparts forms a pear shape round the old town centre. The author Jean Giono was born here, and many of his novels are filled with lyrical descriptions of the countryside round Forcalquier and Banon.

*The old fortified village of Banon is perched on a rocky spur between the Lure and the Lubéron.*

*Following page - Valensole, in the heart of the plateau of the same name, is framed by fragrant fields of lavender.*

MIEL
MIEL
RESTAURANT

In Forcalquier, history comes alive. The town's name, a corruption of Fort Calquier, is a reminder that it is built on a calcareous limestone hill. The town was the capital of Provence in the days when part of the family of the Counts of Provence lived here in the twelfth century, and as a result has a magnificent architectural heritage. The medieval centre was built around the cathedral of Notre-Dame-du-Bourguet, which has a Romanesque nave and a Gothic apse.

Among the town's other architectural curiosities are an astonishing fourteenth-century Gothic fountain in place Saint-Michel and the intimate chapel of Notre-Dame-de-Provence on the terrace of the former citadel.

*Preceding page - Aiguines, at the northern tip of the upper Var, lies at an altitude of 820 metres above the Lac de Sainte-Croix.*

*Between Apt and Banon, the historic village of Simiane-la-Rotonde owes its name to a powerful feudal family, and to the mysterious twelfth-century rotunda that stands over the village.*

Further to the north-west, the little town of Banon is charming indeed. A stroll through the maze of streets between ancient medieval stone walls is an inviting prospect. A narrow street leads up to the fortified entrance of the upper part of the town. There, the Renaissance façades and heavy carved wooden doors of the rue Vieille have been ageing gracefully for centuries beneath the rib-vaulted roof that covers the street.

And now we are nearly back where we started, in the Drôme where the Pre-Alps begin. It has been a whirlwind trip through some of the most enchanting towns and villages in Provence, a brief taste of the treasures, both natural and cultural, that make this region such a magical place.

*Lavender honey on sale in a shop selling local produce in Valensole. Similar shops are to be found in villages all over Provence.*

*Following page - Bauduen, on the shores of the Lac de Sainte-Croix, has a pretty little port and a superb twelfth-century church.*

# Land and sea

Provence is a land of contrasts, lapped by the waters of the Mediterranean and bordered by the mighty Alps. Its gloriously sunny climate entices visitors, and the mistral sometimes chases them away again. "Mistral" means "master" in Provençal, and it really does rule the skies, as the farmers depend on it to sweep all the rain-clouds from the horizon.

The mistral has also helped shape the landscape. The rows of poplars that are the essence of the Provençal countryside were planted for shelter. As the mistral sucks all the moisture from the ground, the farmers have been forced to turn to hardy crops such as vines and olive trees. The shrubs and grasses of the garrigue, or scrubland, have been naturally selected to cope with the bone-dry conditions of the plains.

Yet Provence is also a generous region full of corners of breath-taking beauty, which it sometimes delights in revealing to the unwary visitor like a sultry Provençal beauty flirting with a lover.

*Preceding page - a dry-stone mazet set in a lavender field, its walls glowing in the warm Provençal sun.*

*The calanques of En-Vau, between Cassis and Marseilles.*

The rich soil of Provence grows an abundance of magnificent produce: strawberries from Carpentras, muscat grapes from Mont Ventoux, melons from Cavaillon, cherries from the Comtat, asparagus from Lauris and Mormoiron. The Vaucluse richly deserves its reputation as the market garden of France. It is the country's biggest producer of a whole range of fruit and vegetables, from eating grapes (as opposed to grapes for wine-making), pears, cherries, and courgettes, to garlic, white onions, and melons. It ranks second as a producer of tomatoes, strawberries, and asparagus.

And of course, Provence would not be Provence without the olive, a indispensable part of the landscape. The two key olive-growing areas are round the town of Nyons and in the Alpilles. Here, the olive oil mills often still press the golden nectar as they have always done, grinding the olives between heavy granite millstones.

*Cherries from the Comtat and olives from the Alpilles—a taste of Provence.*

*Following page - Olive trees and sunflowers against the backdrop of an azure sky: the colours of Provence.*

Nature paints Provence with a palette of glorious, intense colours, which have fired the imagination of artists for centuries. Vincent Van Gogh felt drawn to the cheerful, magnificent yellow of the sunflowers when he set down his easel in Arles.

On August 15th, 1888, he wrote to his brother Theo in a state of excitement: "I am painting with the enthusiasm of a son of Marseilles eating his bouillabaisse, which won't surprise you when I tell you I'm painting huge sunflowers". The letter describes three paintings he was working on of the enormous yellow flowers known locally simply as soleils (suns).

*Preceding page and above - Some of Van Gogh's greatest masterpieces were inspired by sunflowers. Whether viewed from above or from the roadside, a field of these superb yellow flowers is always a magnificent sight.*

Provence is also a haven for florists and amateur botanists. In the spring time, the fields are a riot of colour: the deep red of the poppies rivals with the shocking pink or virginal white of the blossom on the cherry trees and in the pear and almond orchards.

Sometimes, visitors are lucky to come across a field of trees all in flower at the same time, like the cherry orchards round Apt.

*Above and following page - The poppy is the king of the field in Provence.*

The true colour of Provence, however, is the intense mauve of the lavender flower, the essence of the countryside. It flowers all summer through, carpeting the landscape with its vividly coloured stripes.

The author Jean Gioni called lavender "the soul of Haute-Provence" and often sang the praises of the "blue of the hills".

*This humble mazet in a vineyard at the foot of Mont Ventoux captures all the magical colours of autumn in Provence.*

*Following page - Nature is the greatest artist of all. Here, she has chosen a palette of red poppies splashed on a background of purple lavender.*

Lavender has always grown wild in Provence. It is only since the end of the nineteenth century that its potential as a commercial crop has been harnessed. Since then it has been farmed intensively for the perfume and soap industries. A hybrid strain, called lavandin, has been bred and is now grown all over the region from Mont Ventoux to Verdon, from the countryside round Sault to the Valensole plateau. The parallel stripes of blue against the brown soil are one of the most characteristic images of Provence.

It is possible to plan a whole holiday round the theme of lavender, from perfume distilleries to lavender gardens and soap factories. There is even an entire museum devoted to lavender in Coustellet, between Cavaillon and Apt, with an exhibition of copper perfume stills dating from the sixteenth century and a short film recounting the history of lavender farming and perfumery in the region. These little purple flowers with their penetrating, heady scent were the fortune of many a Provençal farmer.

*Preceding page - The author Jean Giono called lavender the "soul of Haute-Provence".*

*A Provençal landscape resembling an abstract masterpiece, a tangle of intersecting and parallel lines.*

*Lavender brightens up the Provençal summer with its colourful stripes.*

*Following page - The ochre quarries round Roussillon display an infinite range of warm, spicy tones, from ginger to paprika.*

Lavender purple is not the only colour associated with Provence. The region is also famous for its ochre soil, in the triangle formed by the three villages of Roussillon, Rustrel, and Gargas.

The ochre quarries here are open to the sky, and the sight of the dunes of ochre soil, in an infinite range of nuances from copper to honey, is truly breathtaking, especially in the twilight of a sunny summer evening.

The ochre rocks, with their warm, spicy colours, from saffron to paprika, have been mined here since the end of the eighteenth century. The ochre quarries brought wealth to the small village of Roussillon, until in 1930, industrial dyes and pigments gained the upper hand.

In Roussillon, every façade is washed with a different shade of ochre. One of the old pigment factories now houses an institute devoted to researching ochre and other natural pigments, with a small shop selling samples for artists and for home decoration. A tour of the institute gives a fascinating insight into this unique industrial heritage.

The mountains of Provence look haughtily down on the plains that stretch at their feet. The Lubéron chain is covered in thick woodland, while the Alpilles are a bare expanse of white rock.

Mont Sainte-Victoire, which casts its shadow over Aix-en-Provence, was painted a number of times by Paul Cézanne. Perhaps the most famous of all is Mont Ventoux, climbed by the Italian poet Petrarch in 1336, and today a wonderfully rich nature reserve. In some years, its peace is disturbed by the cyclists of the Tour de France who, in the most gruelling leg of the whole race, must pedal their way up to the summit, 1,912 metres in altitude.

*Preceding page - Dawn light on Mont Ventoux: a palette of blue shades.*

*A hut standing forlorn at the foot of Mont Ventoux after a snowfall.*

Climbing up Mont Ventoux, visitors encounter a number of different ecosystems, from the Mediterranean landscape at the bottom to the Alpine flora and fauna at the summit. The plant life is incredibly varied, from olive trees on the lower slopes to the Rhaetian poppy at the top.

It is also home to a wide range of animals, such as roe deer and wild boar, chamois and mouflon, peregrine falcons and golden eagles. The red deer was reintroduced to the wild here in 1954. In the last days of September, the low, raucous, booming call of the stag may be heard in the distance by a fortunate few.

*Cherry trees in blossom in the Comtat Venaissin.*

*Following page - It rarely snows in Provence. But when it does, the dusting of white over the colours of winter makes for a stunning spectacle.*

*Preceding page - A country footpath on Mont Ventoux at the break of day.*

*Mont Ventoux is listed by UNESCO as an outstanding natural biosphere. Visitors may be fortunate enough to catch a glimpse of roe deer, chamois, or wild stags.*

Provence is also a land of plains. The Crau plain is a dry expanse covered in pebbles left behind by the river Durance in the days when it still flowed as far as the Mediterranean. Stretching from the Camargue to the Etang de Berre (a coastal lake), it resembles a corner of the immense, arid steppes of Central Asia—an impression strengthened by the herds of sheep that come to graze here before the shepherds move them to the Alps for the summer months.

Since an irrigation system was dug for the northern part of the Crau plain in the sixteenth century, it has also been a major hay producer. It was the first region to be awarded an appellation d'origine contrôlée quality label for a crop destined for animal fodder.

*Preceding page and facing - A mountainous landscape in Haute-Provence, near Sault, at the foot of Mont Ventoux. Sheep farming has been going on here for centuries.*

The Camargue is even more immense. It covers an area of some eighty-five thousand hectares to the south of Arles, from Aigues-Mortes to Port-Saint-Louis-de-Rhône. It was granted special protection as a regional natural park in 1967.

The landscape of salt marshes, swamps, and rice paddies make the Camargue a paradise for wild horses and bulls, and for flamingos. It plays a vital role in providing a resting place for the countless millions of migrating birds who stop here on their epic flight from northern Europe to the warmer climes of Africa.

In the Camargue, water is everywhere, from the huge coastal lake of Vacarès and its lacy frill of tiny islands, to the Mediterranean where the land melts into the endless expanse of the sea and the sky.

*How many flamingos are there in this photograph? Count again.*
*The bird on the right has folded its head along its left flank. The head on the right belongs to a third individual. And of course, each bird is standing on one leg.*

*Following page - Camargue horses run wild in the marshes.*
*Some are solitary, others prefer to gallop in herds.*

And so we arrive at the coast. Provence dips its feet in the delicious waters of the Mediterranean all year round. The coast takes on a different character on either side of Marseilles. To the west is the Blue Coast, south of the Estaque hills, a filigree of lakes and sandy spits of land. The resorts of Sausset-les-Pins, Niolon, and Carry-le-Rouet have their own rocky creeks and tempting sandy beaches. To the east, between Marseilles and Cassis, are the calanques—blinding white limestone creeks plunging sheer into emerald waves.

The sixteen kilometres of the calanques form one of the most stunning stretches of coastline anywhere along the Mediterranean basin. The creeks have names: Callelongue, Sormiou, Morgiou, En-Vau, Port-Miou, Port-Pin. The sloping cliffs, reeking of pine resin, lead down to beach huts and tiny marinas with mooring for a few yachts. They are a magical place, offering opportunities for walks, rock climbing, swimming, and scuba diving.

*The calanques of Port-Miou are extremely popular with holidaymakers and scuba divers.*

*Following page - The calanques of Port-Pin are a corner of heaven on earth, with their crystal-clear emerald water.*

Provence is a land of the four elements: earth, air, fire, and water. The region is bounded on three sides by water—the Mediterranean to the south, the Rhône to the west, and the Verdon to the east—while the Durance crosses it in a curving path through Haute-Provence, the Vaucluse, and Bouches-du-Rhône. There are also countless smaller waterways, like the mountain streams that rush down to the plains, such as the refreshingly chilly waters of the Toulourenc that boil in their rocky bed between the Drôme and the Vaucluse.

There is the mysterious spring in Fontaine-de-Vaucluse that wells up in the Vallis Clausa, the narrow valley that gave the Vaucluse its name. The spring, which feeds the river Sorgue, is one of the most abundant in the world. Nobody knows how deep the fountainhead of the spring lies. The waters well up to the surface at the foot of a cliff that stands 230 metres tall. The inexhaustible waters of this mysterious spring are of a limpid, emerald green. The secret of its source is just another of the mysteries of Provence that make the region such an endlessly fascinating and charming place to visit—or to live.

*Preceding page - The grandiose spectacle of the Verdon gorges.*

*Fontaine-de-Vaucluse, in a mysterious narrow valley, where the river Sorgue takes its source.*

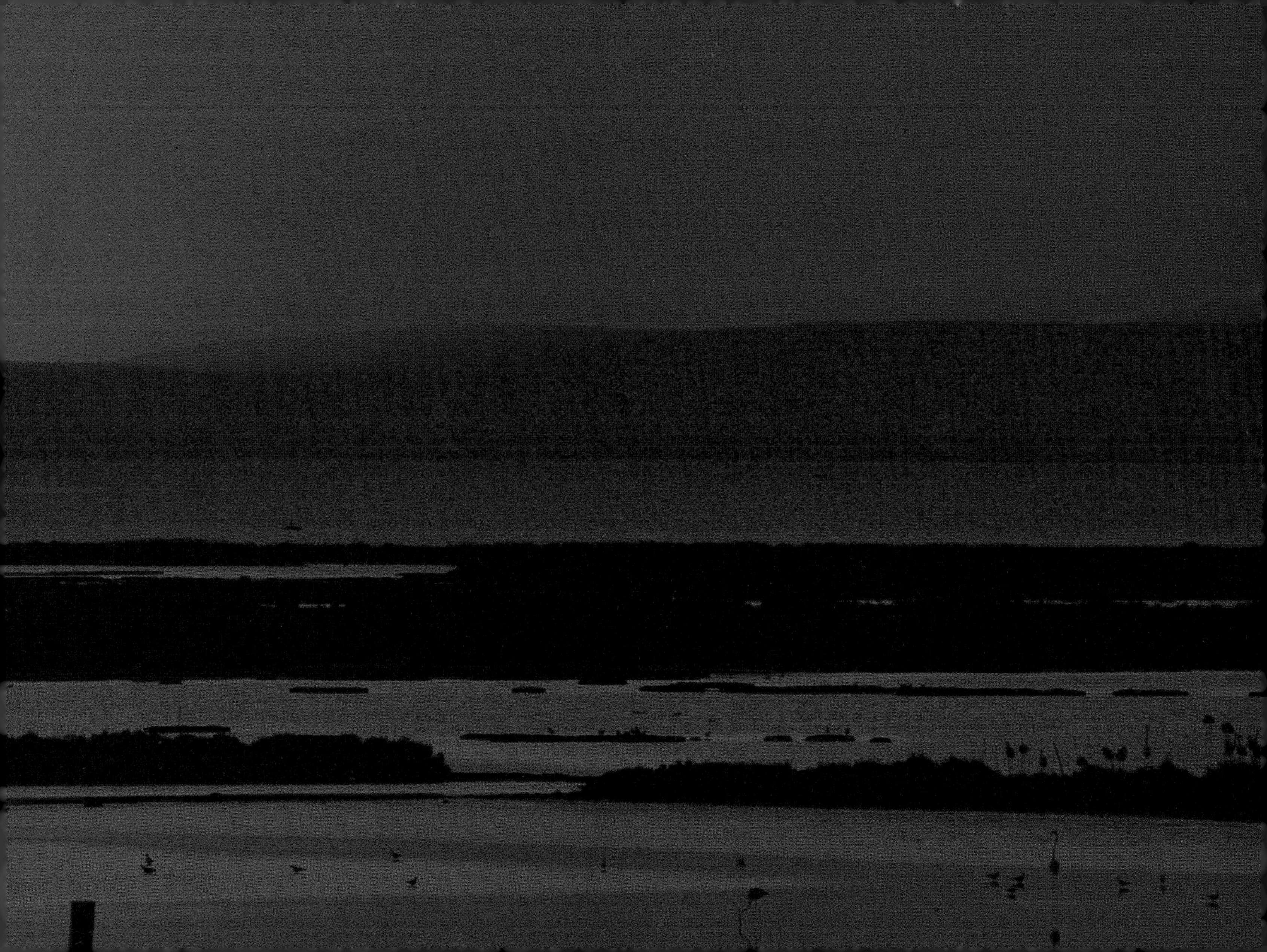

RESTAURANT
les opticiens
V.T.L

# Provençal traditions

Myths and rituals, folk tales and traditions whose origins are shrouded in the mists of time, local legends and customs—the ancestral Provençal way of life is still alive and going strong in many parts of this region.

The passing of the seasons is marked by feast days that provide an opportunity for the hard-working farmers to give thanks for the bounty of the soil. The feast day of Saint Eloi, patron saint of peasants and blacksmiths, is celebrated from Marseilles to Châteaurenard and in the Alpilles with processions of carts decorated with branches, garlands of flowers, and fruits, pulled by horses with brightly coloured bridles.

*Preceding page - Locals celebrating the feast day of Saint Eloi in Châteaurenard to the sound of drums.*

*A beautiful Sévillane riding a Camargue horse, accompanied by an attentive young man.*

Christmas holds a special place in the hearts of many Provençal men and women. A legend passed down through the centuries says that the Infant Jesus was in fact born here. The end-of-year festivities are commemorated with a huge meal rounded off with thirteen traditional desserts in reference to the twelve disciples and Jesus. Crib scenes recreating the birth of Jesus in the stable, complete with shepherds, the three wise men, and animals, are also a traditional feature of a Provençal Christmas. The small terracotta figurines are called santons, a name derived from the Provençal santoun, meaning "little saints". The first santons were made during the French Revolution in 1789. Since all the churches were closed, the Marseilles sculptor Jean-Louis Lagnel decided to create miniature crib scenes for people to have in their homes instead.

To begin with, only figurines illustrating Bible scenes were produced, but as the idea caught on, sculptors began producing figurines representing traditional Provençal characters and trades, such as the knife grinder, the blacksmith, the tambourin player, and the fishwife.

*A santon representing the figure of Paul Cézanne, the artist, born in Aix.*

*Mireille Fouque's family has been making santons in Aix-en-Provence for three generations.*

*"The mistral is blowing", a 1952 model made by the Fouque family.*

Provence is also famed for its traditional fabric printed with sprigs of flowers and other popular motifs. The fashion began with the Indian cotton fabrics that arrived in the port of Marseilles from the seventeenth century onwards, and in fact the fabric is still known as indienne.

The brightly coloured cloth—golden yellow, grenadine red, cobalt blue—is printed with flowers or geometric patterns. It is often used for the padded eiderdowns stitched with intricate patterns called boutis, and for the traditional costumes that many Provençal men and women born and bred will wear with pride on important feast days.

*Preceding page - A Provençal skirt made of Indian cotton. This style has been traditional in the region since the seventeenth century.*

*Women from Arles dressed up in their traditional costume for a feast day.*

The traditional outfit worn by women from Arles is typical of the region, consisting in a long coloured skirt, a bodice with tight sleeves, a neckerchief in white lace or in the same fabric as the skirt covering the tulle front of the blouse, and a very distinctive head-dress, with ribbons wrapped round an elaborate hairstyle.

This is the traditional costume that visitors now are most likely to see, as it is still widely worn by women in Arles for the numerous feast days celebrated in Arles itself and in the Camargue.

Visitors have a good chance to see the delightful sight of a crowd of Arlésiennes in traditional garb at one of the frequent férias—a great local tradition—which would not be complete without a bull run through the streets with a crowd of young men showing off their bravado as they chase behind. The wild Camargue bulls are an important part of local traditions, and many towns here have their own bull-fighting arena.

*A group of young women in traditional outfits from the Comtat and Arles.*

*Facing and following page - Les belles Arlésiennes.*

France Bleu

The arena in Arles hosts regular courses camarguaises as well as Spanish-style bull-fighting. In the course camarguaise, the aim is not to plant the final death blow, but rather to snatch a rosette attached between the bull's razor-sharp horns. This of course requires great agility and nerves of steel. The razeteur must run round the bull in a circle and attempt to snatch the rosette without being gored.

Spanish corridas were first held in Provence in the mid nineteenth century, and still attract crowds of many thousands of aficionados every year from April to September.

While the crowds roar their encouragement to the razeteurs inside the arena, the streets outside are partying too. Rows of bodegas have been set up for the féria, the sangria and local wines flow freely, and the locals dance the sévillanne to the rhythm of the peñas—boisterous groups of street musicians whose trumpets set everyone's feet tapping.

*Preceding page - The Arles arena, which often rings with the enthusiastic shouts of the crowd at a course camarguaise.*

*An intrepid razeteur snatching a rosette from between the horns of a wild bull.*

*A bullfighter presenting the muleta, or cape.*

This brings us to another indispensable Provençal tradition—the apéritif! The long, hot days make the thought of a cool drink with tinkling ice cubes in the early evening as the heat begins to die down enticing indeed.

The favourite is pastis, or pastaga as the locals call it: a refreshing golden aniseed liquor that goes cloudy when water is added. There are a number of local recipes and brands, each with a varying combination of herbs to give a subtly different taste. There is nothing to beat sitting at a shady café terrace watching the world go by, with a glass of pastis to hand to wash down a dish of fat, shiny black olives, toast smeared with a thick layer of tapenade (olive paste), and handfuls of salty grilled almonds.

Pastis is much beloved of the old men who spend whole days playing petanque in the village square.

*Pastis, liqueur wine, and a dish of black olives—the perfect apéritif.*

Petanque, like pastis, is a regional speciality that has proved popular all over France. It is said that the game was invented by a certain Jules Le Noir from La Ciotat, who had lost the use of his legs. Since he could not take a run up to throw the boules as the traditional version of the game from Lyons required, he threw them from a standing position, feet together, "pé tanco" in Provençal—hence the name petanque.

The new version of the game spread like wildfire. Now there cannot be a single village in all of Provence that does not have a special strip of flattened earth specially for playing petanque—and it is certain that in Provence, few things cause passions to run higher than an argument about whose boule knocked whose out of the way!

*Pétanque is played with deadly seriousness in villages all over Provence.*

MYRTILLE
1,90 € LES 50g
2,00 € LES 50g
1,50 € LES 50g
1,50 € LES 50g
PRELE
1,10 € LES 50g
1,40 € LES
CAMOMILLE ROMAINE
2,30 € LES 25g
BRUYERE
1,40 € LES 50g
FRENE
1,20 € LES 50g
ORTIE BLANCHE
2,20 € LES 50g
COMBRETUM
1,90 € LES 50g
EUCALYPTUS
1,30 € LES 50g
PISSENLIT
4,80 € LES 100g
HAMAMELIS
2,30 € LES 50g
CAMOMILLE MATRICAIRE
ORTIE PIQUANTE
1,20 € LES 50g
COQUELICOT
1,60 € LES 25g
VIGNE ROUGE
1,50 € LES 50g
BARDANE
1,60 € LES 50g
GINKOBILOBA
1,50 € LES 50g
BOLDO
ARMOISE
1,70 € LES 50g
MILLEFEUILLE
1,40 € LES 50g
BOUILLON BLANC
1,50 € LES 50g

# Gastronomy

Provence's culinary traditions are as varied as the land itself, which is hardly surprising, considering the bounteous produce that the farmers are blessed with.

Provençal cuisine is rich in savours, and the delicious local herbs give a wonderful variety of dishes. Certain ingredients immediately call up visions of the lavender-scented hills of Provence. Olive oil is one of these: tasty and with near-miraculous health-giving properties, it is used for seasoning, basting, frying, or simply to bring out the taste of dishes.

A simple salad of tomatoes, garlic, and basil with a splash of olive oil is heaven—and what would bouillabaisse be without it? It is equally delicious with fresh goat's cheese, a mullet roasted on a barbecue, or even drizzled over an apple tart.

*Preceding page - Local herbs and spices bring out the best in Provençal cuisine.*

*Carpentras strawberries with candied olives and red berries from the Vaucluse, as a mousse with basil gelée or as a sorbet —a culinary treat invented by Michel Del Burgo.*

Olive oil is so symbolic of Mediterranean cuisine and the sun-drenched landscape where it grows that specialists describe it in terms of grand crus and cépages, just as if it were a fine wine.

The cépage depends on the variety of olive used: salonique, tanche, verdale, picholine, or berruguette. Each olive oil has its own distinct personality, as varied as the tones of green or gold when the sun shines through the bottle. Some are fruity and soft, while others are slightly bitter, with a bouquet of dried fruits, artichokes, or roasted pear. The most reputed oils are produced in Les Baux-de-Provence, Nyons, the Comtat, and in the countryside round Aix.

*Traditional Provençal cuisine is not only delicious—it is also very healthy, thanks to the virtues of olive oil.*

Provence also has an enviable reputation for its wines. Vineyards glow gold in the setting sun all along the Rhône valley. The best côtes-du-rhônes are a byword for great wine the world over: châteauneuf-du-pape, gigondas, vacqueyras, cairanne.

The other wine-producing areas are also worth exploring: côtes-de-ventoux, côtes-du-lubéron, and côtes-de-provence, not forgetting the full-bodied vintages of Cassis and Bandol along the coast.

*Muscat de Beaumes-de-Venise, tavel,
and other côtes-du-rhône grands crus on sale
at the Bouteillerie du Palais des Papes in Avignon.*

Fine fresh Provençal produce is at its best with a drizzle of olive oil and accompanied by a glass of rich ruby-red wine.

The region is renowned for its abundance of fruit and vegetables ripened by the generous warmth of the sun, the aromatic herbs that grow wild in the garrigue, deliciously tender lamb fattened on the slopes of Mont Ventoux, fresh-caught fish and seafood sold daily in the ports, ripe, pungent banon and picodon goat's cheese (from Haute-Provence and the Drôme), and rustic spelt wheat from the countryside round Sault, which has recently come back into fashion thanks to the efforts of a few great chefs passionate about traditional Provençal cuisine.

*Tender, tasty lamb from Ventoux or the countryside round the town of Sault is a speciality of many of the finest restaurants in Provence.*

Among the most ardent defenders of Provençal cooking is Michel Del Burgo, who began learning the secrets of his art almost as soon as he could walk. He served his apprenticeship with two great masters of Provençal cuisine, Raymond Thuillier and Jean-André Charial in Les Baux-de-Provence, before setting out to earn a few accolades of his own. Now, at the age of forty, he is back in Provence after a few years in Paris. In 2003, he took over the kitchens in the restaurant that now bears his name in La Bastide, Gordes.

His richly inventive, self-expressive style there draws its inspiration from traditional Mediterranean, and more particularly Provençal, cuisine. He enjoys experimenting with local ingredients to create such dishes as green-tipped asparagus from Lauris with fresh coriander pistou (the Provençal version of pesto) served with black olive bread croustilles, risotto made with spelt wheat from Sault with black truffles, or roasted tender young pigeons from Alpes-de-Haute-Provence

*Lauris asparagus with orange sabayon and coriander pistou, prepared by the talented chef Michel Del Burgo (pictured opposite), who recently took over the kitchens of La Bastide in Gordes.*

The rich culinary heritage of Provence has a number of chefs who are proud to work with the finest local produce. Christian Etienne, now based in Avignon, makes superb dishes with simple, fresh ingredients such as tomatoes, olive oil, and rabasse—the local name for truffles. The finest specimens grow in a triangle formed by the three towns of Tricastin, Carpentras, and Richerenches—known as the capital of the truffle because of its celebrated weekly truffle market. Other Provençal chefs also specialise in this magical fungus. Among the best are Guy Jullien in Mondragon, and Michel Philibert in Monteux.

At Le Prieuré, in Villeneuve-lès-Avignon, Serge Chenet delights in combining the most carefully selected of ingredients to concoct a cuisine that explodes with flavour. He especially enjoys throwing together unexpected combinations, often ending up with a match made in heaven, such as a light-as-air lobster and leek mousse flavoured with liquorice, fillet of mullet on a crispy horseradish pancake, tapenade madeleines, and basil and lavender sorbets that capture the essence of Provence.

*Serge Chenet has won awards for his innovative cuisine. He is the head chef at Le Prieuré, in Villeneuve-lès-Avignon.*

In Cavaillon, Jean-Jacques Prévôt has devoted his skills to the town's best-known export—melons. He uses them in numerous ingenious recipes, from starters to desserts. At the Moulin de Lourmarin, the chef Edouard Loubet has a particular love of aromatic plants and herbs and old-fashioned vegetables, which he combines to bring the flavours of bygone days back to life. Reine Sammut is the only female chef in Provence to have been awarded a star in the indispensable Michelin restaurant guide. Again, she specialises in local produce, and the meals she serves in her restaurant, La Fenière in Lourmarin, are a poem in praise of traditional Provençal cuisine.

We finish with one of the greatest chefs of the whole of the south of France, Jean-André Charial. His magical, almost mythical restaurant, L'Oustau de Baumanière in Les Baux-de-Provence, serves the very freshest seafood from the waters of the Mediterranean, fruit and vegetables gently ripened by the warmth of the Provençal sun, wild herbs straight from the garrigue, and lamb and rabbit bred locally.

*Jean-André Charial is one of the most talented chefs working in the Provençal tradition. He cooks at L'Oustau de Baumanière in Les Baux-de-Provence.*

*Bass with capers and taggiasche olives and a Baux-de-Provence wine jus.*
*This appetising Provençal speciality is on the menu at L'Oustau de Baumanière.*

*Following page - Olives can be served in a variety of ways,*
*plain or stuffed à la provençale.*

These pages would not be complete without a quick look at some typical Provençal dishes. Perhaps the best known is bouillabaisse, a thick, chunky fish soup invented by Marseilles fishermen to use up the fish from their catch they had not managed to sell. Then there are pieds-paquets, also from Marseilles, a dish consisting of a mixture of sheep's feet and stuffed tripe simmered with bacon, onions, garlic, carrots, and white wine, and the deliciously hearty soupe au pistou, based on diced fresh vegetables and white haricot beans mixed with pistou—a paste of crushed basil, garlic, and olive oil—for flavour.

You might also be offered stuffed baby vegetables, aïoli—garlic mayonnaise, often served with cod and steamed vegetables—a daube, or stew, of beef or Camargue bull, tomatoes à la provençale, oven-baked with a topping of garlic, parsley, and breadcrumbs and a drizzle of olive oil, and finally, the unforgettable ratatouille—a stew of tomatoes, courgettes, aubergines, and red pepper gently browned in garlic-flavoured olive oil. All the flavours of Provence explode together with every mouthful.

VERTE
DENOYAUTÉE
LA PROVENÇALE
2€5 les 250 grs
HUILE D'OLIVE
Vierge Extra
FAÇON
KALAMATA
2€5 les 250 grs
Château Virant
PANOUZE
TAHITIENNE
2€5 les 250 grs
LA NYONS

For dessert, you might like to try calissons from Aix-en-Provence—a paste of ground almonds and candied melon with an icing sugar coating. Apt is well-known for its candied fruits, which have been made there since medieval times. Candying consists in replacing the water content of the fruit with sugar syrup, which can take several weeks. It is said that the popes of Avignon were very fond of candied fruit.

Berlingots were probably invented in the mid nineteenth century by a confectioner from Carpentras who decided to experiment with the sugar syrup left after cooking candied fruit. He added mint, a very popular flavour in those days, and legend has it that because of their shape, he named the sweets after the Provençal version of the game of jacks, berlingaù.

*Candied fruit from Apt. This tradition is kept alive today by a few master confectioners, such as Denis Ceccon at Le Coulon, in Apt.*

*Right page - Carpentras berlingots, stripy boiled sweets made from the sugar syrup left over from candying fruit.*

*Following pages - Calissons from Aix, made from candied melon and marzipan.*

14, rue des Volontaires - 75015 Paris
**Tel.** (33) 1 53 69 70 00 - **Fax** (33) 1 42 73 15 24
**E-mail :** *contact@declics.fr*

**Printed by** Corlet, Condé-sur-Noireau (14) - N° 71223
**Distribution** Nouveau Quartier Latin
**Dépôt légal** 2nd quarter 2003
**ISBN Code** 2-84768-046-2

*Following double spread - Olive trees and sunflowers.*

*Back cover - a dry-stone mazet in a field of lavender, caressed by the warm Provençal sun.*